A STREET
IN BRONZEVILLE

BY

GWENDOLYN BROOKS

HARPER & BROTHERS PUBLISHERS

NEW YORK and LONDON

1945

TO MY PARENTS

DAVID AND KEZIAH

———

8-5   THIRD EDITION   K-U

CONTENTS

A STREET
IN BRONZEVILLE

the old-marrieds

BUT in the crowding darkness not a word did they say.
Though the pretty-coated birds had piped so lightly all
the day.
And he had seen the lovers in the little side-streets.
And she had heard the morning stories clogged with
sweets.
It was quite a time for loving. It was midnight. It was
May.
But in the crowding darkness not a word did they say.

kitchenette building

WE ARE things of dry hours and the involuntary plan,
Grayed in, and gray. "Dream" makes a giddy sound, not
      strong
Like "rent," "feeding a wife," "satisfying a man."

But could a dream send up through onion fumes
Its white and violet, fight with fried potatoes
And yesterday's garbage ripening in the hall,
Flutter, or sing an aria down these rooms

Even if we were willing to let it in,
Had time to warm it, keep it very clean,
Anticipate a message, let it begin?

We wonder. But not well! not for a minute!
Since Number Five is out of the bathroom now,
We think of lukewarm water, hope to get in it.

the mother

ABORTIONS will not let you forget.
You remember the children you got that you did not
    get,
The damp small pulps with a little or with no hair,
The singers and workers that never handled the air.
You will never neglect or beat
Them, or silence or buy with a sweet.
You will never wind up the sucking-thumb
Or scuttle off ghosts that come.
You will never leave them, controlling your luscious
    sigh,
Return for a snack of them, with gobbling mother-eye.

I have heard in the voices of the wind the voices of my
    dim killed children.
I have contracted. I have eased
My dim dears at the breasts they could never suck.
I have said, Sweets, if I sinned, if I seized
Your luck
And your lives from your unfinished reach,
If I stole your births and your names,
Your straight baby tears and your games,
Your stilted or lovely loves, your tumults, your mar-
    riages, aches, and your deaths,
If I poisoned the beginnings of your breaths,
Believe that even in my deliberateness I was not de-
    liberate.
Though why should I whine,

Whine that the crime was other than mine?—
Since anyhow you are dead.
Or rather, or instead,
You were never made.
But that too, I am afraid,
Is faulty: oh, what shall I say, how is the truth to be
    said?
You were born, you had body, you died.
It is just that you never giggled or planned or cried.

Believe me, I loved you all.
Believe me, I knew you, though faintly, and I loved, I
    loved you
All.

southeast corner

THE School of Beauty's a tavern now.
The Madam is underground.
Out at Lincoln, among the graves
Her own is early found.
Where the thickest, tallest monument
Cuts grandly into the air
The Madam lies, contentedly.
Her fortune, too, lies there,
Converted into cool hard steel
And bright red velvet lining;
While over her tan impassivity
Shot silk is shining.

when Mrs. Martin's Booker T.

WHEN Mrs. Martin's Booker T.
Ruined Rosa Brown
Mrs. Martin moved away
To the low west side of town.
"Don't care if I never see that boy
Again to the end of my days.
He wrung my heart like a chicken neck.
And he made me a disgrace.
Don't come to tell me he's dyin'.
Don't come to tell me he's dead.
But tell me if'n he take that gal
And get her decent wed."

the soft man

DISGUSTING, isn't it, dealing out the damns
To every comer? Hits the heart like pain.
And calling women (Marys) chicks and broads,
Men hep, and cats, or corny to the jive.
Being seen Everywhere (keeping Alive),
Rhumboogie (and the joint is jumpin', Joe),
Brass Rail, Keyhole, De Lisa, Cabin Inn.
And all the other garbage cans.

But grin.
Because there is a clean unanxious place
To which you creep on Sundays. And you cool
In lovely sadness.

No one giggles where
You bathe your sweet vulgarity in prayer.

the funeral

To WHATEVER you incline, your final choice here must
be handling
Occasional sweet clichés with a dishonesty of deft tact.
For these people are stricken, they want none of your
long-range messages,
Only the sweet clichés, to pamper them, modify fright.
Many friends have sent flowers, clubs have been kind
with sprays,
Wreaths. The flowers provide a kind of heat. Sick
Thick odor-loveliness winds nicely about the shape of
mourning,
A dainty horror. People think of flowers upon rot—
And for moments together the corpse is no colder than
they.
They glance at each other, want love from each other:
Or they do not glance but out of tight eyes vaguely pray.

Preacher and tradition of piety and propriety rise. The
people wait
For the dear blindfold: "Heaven is Good denied.
Rich are the men who have died."

hunchback girl: she thinks of heaven

MY FATHER, it is surely a blue place
And straight. Right. Regular. Where I shall find
No need for scholarly nonchalance or looks
A little to the left or guards upon the
Heart to halt love that runs without crookedness
Along its crooked corridors. My Father,
It is a planned place surely. Out of coils,
Unscrewed, released, no more to be marvelous,
I shall walk straightly through most proper halls
Proper myself, princess of properness.

a song in the front yard

I've stayed in the front yard all my life.
I want a peek at the back
Where it's rough and untended and hungry weed grows.
A girl gets sick of a rose.

I want to go in the back yard now
And maybe down the alley,
To where the charity children play.
I want a good time today.

They do some wonderful things.
They have some wonderful fun.
My mother sneers, but I say it's fine
How they don't have to go in at quarter to nine.
My mother, she tells me that Johnnie Mae
Will grow up to be a bad woman.
That George'll be taken to Jail soon or late
(On account of last winter he sold our back gate.)

But I say it's fine. Honest, I do.
And I'd like to be a bad woman, too,
And wear the brave stockings of night-black lace
And strut down the streets with paint on my face.

patent leather

THAT cool chick down on Calumet
Has got herself a brand new cat,
With pretty patent-leather hair.
And he is man enough for her.

Us other guys don't think he's such
A much.
His voice is shrill.
His muscle is pitiful.

That cool chick down on Calumet,
Though, says he's really "it."
And strokes the patent-leather hair
That makes him man enough for her.

the ballad of chocolate Mabbie

IT WAS Mabbie without the grammar school gates.
And Mabbie was all of seven.
And Mabbie was cut from a chocolate bar.
And Mabbie thought life was heaven.

The grammar school gates were the pearly gates,
For Willie Boone went to school.
When she sat by him in history class
Was only her eyes were cool.

It was Mabbie without the grammar school gates
Waiting for Willie Boone.
Half hour after the closing bell!
He would surely be coming soon.

Oh, warm is the waiting for joys, my dears!
And it cannot be too long.
Oh, pity the little poor chocolate lips
That carry the bubble of song!

Out came the saucily bold Willie Boone.
It was woe for our Mabbie now.
He wore like a jewel a lemon-hued lynx
With sand-waves loving her brow.

It was Mabbie alone by the grammar school gates.
Yet chocolate companions had she:
Mabbie on Mabbie with hush in the heart.
Mabbie on Mabbie to be.

the preacher: ruminates behind the sermon

I THINK it must be lonely to be God.
Nobody loves a master. No. Despite
The bright hosannas, bright dear-Lords, and bright
Determined reverence of Sunday eyes.

Picture Jehovah striding through the hall
Of His importance, creatures running out
From servant-corners to acclaim, to shout
Appreciation of His merit's glare.

But who walks with Him?—dares to take His arm,
To slap Him on the shoulder, tweak His ear,
Buy Him a Coca-Cola or a beer,
Pooh-pooh His politics, call Him a fool?

Perhaps—who knows?—He tires of looking down.
Those eyes are never lifted. Never straight.
Perhaps sometimes He tires of being great
In solitude. Without a hand to hold.

Sadie and Maud

MAUD went to college.
Sadie stayed at home.
Sadie scraped life
With a fine-tooth comb.

She didn't leave a tangle in.
Her comb found every strand.
Sadie was one of the livingest chits
In all the land.

Sadie bore two babies
Under her maiden name.
Maud and Ma and Papa
Nearly died of shame.
Every one but Sadie
Nearly died of shame.

When Sadie said her last so-long
Her girls struck out from home.
(Sadie had left as heritage
Her fine-tooth comb.)

Maud, who went to college,
Is a thin brown mouse.
She is living all alone
In this old house.

14

the independent man

Now who could take you off to tiny life
In one room or in two rooms or in three
And cork you smartly, like the flask of wine
You are? Not any woman. Not a wife.
You'd let her twirl you, give her a good glee
Showing your leaping ruby to a friend.
Though twirling would be meek. Since not a cork
Could you allow, for being made so free.

A woman would be wise to think it well
If once a week you only rang the bell.

obituary for a living lady

MY FRIEND was decently wild
As a child.
And as a young girl
She was interested in a brooch and pink powder and a
    curl.
As a young woman though
She fell in love with a man who didn't know
That even if she wouldn't let him touch her breasts she
    was still worth his hours,
Stopped calling Sundays with flowers.
Sunday after Sunday she put on her clean, gay (though
    white) dress,
Worried the windows. There was so much silence she
    finally decided that the next time she would say
    "yes."
But the man had found by then a woman who dressed
    in red.
My friend spent a hundred weeks or so wishing she were
    dead.
But crying for yourself, when you give it all of your
    time, gets tedious after a while.
Therefore she terminated her mourning, made for her
    mouth a sad sweet smile
And discovered the country of God. Now she will not
    dance
And she thinks not the thinnest thought of any type of
    romance

And I can't get her to take a touch of the best cream
    cologne.
However even without lipstick she is lovely and it is no
    wonder that the preacher (at present) is almost a
    synonym for her telephone
And watches the neutral kind bland eyes that moisten
    the first pew center on Sunday—I beg your pardon
    —Sabbath nights
And wonders as his stomach breaks up into fire and
    lights
How long it will be
Before he can, with reasonably slight risk of rebuke,
    put his hand on her knee.

——And when you have forgotten the bright bedclothes
   on a Wednesday and a Saturday,
And most especially when you have forgotten Sunday—
When you have forgotten Sunday halves in bed,
Or me sitting on the front-room radiator in the limping
   afternoon
Looking off down the long street
To nowhere,
Hugged by my plain old wrapper of no-expectation
And nothing-I-have-to-do and I'm-happy-why?
And if-Monday-never-had-to-come—
When you have forgotten that, I say,
And how you swore, if somebody beeped the bell,
And how my heart played hopscotch if the telephone
   rang;
And how we finally went in to Sunday dinner,
That is to say, went across the front room floor to the
   ink-spotted table in the southwest corner
To Sunday dinner, which was always chicken and
   noodles
Or chicken and rice
And salad and rye bread and tea
And chocolate chip cookies—
I say, when you have forgotten that,
When you have forgotten my little presentiment
That the war would be over before they got to you;
And how we finally undressed and whipped out the
   light and flowed into bed,

18

And lay loose-limbed for a moment in the week-end
Bright bedclothes,
Then gently folded into each other—
When you have, I say, forgotten all that,
Then you may tell,
Then I may believe
You have forgotten me well.

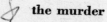 **the murder**

THIS is where poor Percy died,
Short of the age of one.
His brother Brucie, with a grin,
Burned him up for fun.

No doubt, poor Percy watched the fire
Chew on his baby dress
With sweet delight, enjoying too
His brother's happiness.

No doubt, poor Percy looked around
And wondered at the heat,
Was worried, wanted Mother,
Who gossiped down the street.

No doubt, poor shrieking Percy died
Loving Brucie still,
Who could, with clean and open eye,
Thoughtfully kill.

Brucie has no playmates now.
His mother mourns his lack.
Brucie keeps on asking, "When
Is Percy comin' back?"

of De Witt Williams on his way to Lincoln Cemetery

HE WAS born in Alabama.
He was bred in Illinois.
He was nothing but a
Plain black boy.

Swing low swing low sweet sweet chariot.
Nothing but a plain black boy.

Drive him past the Pool Hall.
Drive him past the Show.
Blind within his casket,
But maybe he will know.

Down through Forty-seventh Street:
Underneath the L,
And—Northwest Corner, Prairie,
That he loved so well.

Don't forget the Dance Halls—
Warwick and Savoy,
Where he picked his women, where
He drank his liquid joy.

Born in Alabama.
Bred in Illinois.
He was nothing but a
Plain black boy.

Swing low swing low sweet sweet chariot.
Nothing but a plain black boy.

Matthew Cole

HERE are the facts.
He's sixty-six.
He rooms in a stove-heated flat
Over on Lafayette.
He has roomed there ten years long.
He never will be done
With dust and his ceiling that
Is everlasting sad,
And the gloomy housekeeper
Who forgets to build the fire,
And the red fat roaches that stroll
Unafraid up his wall,
And the whiteless grin of the housekeeper
On Saturday night when he pays his four
Dollars, the ceaseless Sunday row
Of her big cheap radio. . . .

She'll tell you he is the pleasantest man—
Always a smile, a smile. . . . But in
The door-locked dirtiness of his room
He never smiles. Except when come,
Say, thoughts of a little boy licorice-full
Without a nickel for Sunday School.
Or thoughts of a little boy playing ball
And swearing at sound of his mother's call.
Once, I think, he laughed aloud,
At thought of a wonderful joke he'd played
On the whole crowd, the old crowd. . . .

the vacant lot

Mrs. COLEY's three-flat brick
Isn't here any more.
All done with seeing her fat little form
Burst out of the basement door;
And with seeing her African son-in-law
(Rightful heir to the throne)
With his great white strong cold squares of teeth
And his little eyes of stone;
And with seeing the squat fat daughter
Letting in the men
When majesty has gone for the day—
And letting them out again.

THE SUNDAYS
OF SATIN-LEGS SMITH

Inamoratas, with an approbation,
Bestowed his title. Blessed his inclination.)

He wakes, unwinds, elaborately: a cat
Tawny, reluctant, royal. He is fat
And fine this morning. Definite. Reimbursed.

He waits a moment, he designs his reign,
That no performance may be plain or vain.
Then rises in a clear delirium.

He sheds, with his pajamas, shabby days.
And his desertedness, his intricate fear, the
Postponed resentments and the prim precautions.

Now, at his bath, would you deny him lavender
Or take away the power of his pine?
What smelly substitute, heady as wine,
Would you provide? life must be aromatic.
There must be scent, somehow there must be some.
Would you have flowers in his life? suggest
Asters? a Really Good geranium?
A white carnation? would you prescribe a Show
With the cold lilies, formal chrysanthemum
Magnificence, poinsettias, and emphatic
Red of prize roses? might his happiest
Alternative (you muse) be, after all,

24

A bit of gentle garden in the best
Of taste and straight tradition? Maybe so.
But you forget, or did you ever know,
His heritage of cabbage and pigtails,
Old intimacy with alleys, garbage pails,
Down in the deep (but always beautiful) South
Where roses blush their blithest (it is said)
And sweet magnolias put Chanel to shame.

No! He has not a flower to his name.
Except a feather one, for his lapel.
Apart from that, if he should think of flowers
It is in terms of dandelions or death.
Ah, there is little hope. You might as well—
Unless you care to set the world a-boil
And do a lot of equalizing things,
Remove a little ermine, say, from kings,
Shake hands with paupers and appoint them men,
For instance—certainly you might as well
Leave him his lotion, lavender and oil.

Let us proceed. Let us inspect, together
With his meticulous and serious love,
The innards of this closet. Which is a vault
Whose glory is not diamonds, not pearls,
Not silver plate with just enough dull shine.
But wonder-suits in yellow and in wine,
Sarcastic green and zebra-striped cobalt.
All drapes. With shoulder padding that is wide
And cocky and determined as his pride;
Ballooning pants that taper off to ends

25

Scheduled to choke precisely.

                                   Here are hats
Like bright umbrellas; and hysterical ties
Like narrow banners for some gathering war.

People are so in need, in need of help.
People want so much that they do not know.

Below the tinkling trade of little coins
The gold impulse not possible to show
Or spend. Promise piled over and betrayed.

These kneaded limbs receive the kiss of silk.
Then they receive the brave and beautiful
Embrace of some of that equivocal wool.
He looks into his mirror, loves himself—
The neat curve here; the angularity
That is appropriate at just its place;
The technique of a variegated grace.

Here is all his sculpture and his art
And all his architectural design.
Perhaps you would prefer to this a fine
Value of marble, complicated stone.
Would have him think with horror of baroque,
Rococo. You forget and you forget.

He dances down the hotel steps that keep
Remnants of last night's high life and distress.
As spat-out purchased kisses and spilled beer.
He swallows sunshine with a secret yelp.

Passes to coffee and a roll or two.
Has breakfasted.

     Out. Sounds about him smear,
Become a unit. He hears and does not hear
The alarm clock meddling in somebody's sleep;
Children's governed Sunday happiness;
The dry tone of a plane; a woman's oath;
Consumption's spiritless expectoration;
An indignant robin's resolute donation
Pinching a track through apathy and din;
Restaurant vendors weeping; and the L
That comes on like a slightly horrible thought.

Pictures, too, as usual, are blurred.
He sees and does not see the broken windows
Hiding their shame with newsprint; little girl
With ribbons decking wornness, little boy
Wearing the trousers with the decentest patch,
To honor Sunday; women on their way
From "service," temperate holiness arranged
Ably on asking faces; men estranged
From music and from wonder and from joy
But far familiar with the guiding awe
Of foodlessness.

     He loiters.

       Restaurant vendors
Weep, or out of them rolls a restless glee.
The Lonesome Blues, the Long-lost Blues, I Want A
Big Fat Mama. Down these sore avenues
Comes no Saint-Saëns, no piquant elusive Grieg,
And not Tschaikovsky's wayward eloquence

27

And not the shapely tender drift of Brahms.
But could he love them? Since a man must bring
To music what his mother spanked him for
When he was two: bits of forgotten hate,
Devotion: whether or not his mattress hurts:
The little dream his father humored: the thing
His sister did for money: what he ate
For breakfast—and for dinner twenty years
Ago last autumn: all his skipped desserts.

The pasts of his ancestors lean against
Him. Crowd him. Fog out his identity.
Hundreds of hungers mingle with his own,
Hundreds of voices advise so dexterously
He quite considers his reactions his,
Judges he walks most powerfully alone,
That everything is—simply what it is.

But movie-time approaches, time to boo
The hero's kiss, and boo the heroine
Whose ivory and yellow it is sin
For his eye to eat of. The Mickey Mouse,
However, is for everyone in the house.

Squires his lady to dinner at Joe's Eats.
His lady alters as to leg and eye,
Thickness and height, such minor points as these,
From Sunday to Sunday. But no matter what
Her name or body positively she's
In Queen Lace stockings with ambitious heels
That strain to kiss the calves, and vivid shoes

Frontless and backless, Chinese fingernails,
Earrings, three layers of lipstick, intense hat
Dripping with the most voluble of veils.
Her affable extremes are like sweet bombs
About him, whom no middle grace or good
Could gratify. He had no education
In quiet arts of compromise. He would
Not understand your counsels on control, nor
Thank you for your late trouble.

At Joe's Eats

You get your fish or chicken on meat platters.
With coleslaw, macaroni, candied sweets,
Coffee and apple pie. You go out full.
(The end is—isn't it?—all that really matters.)

And even and intrepid come
The tender boots of night to home.

Her body is like new brown bread
Under the Woolworth mignonette.
Her body is a honey bowl
Whose waiting honey is deep and hot.
Her body is like summer earth,
Receptive, soft, and absolute . . .

NEGRO HERO
to suggest Dorie Miller

I HAD to kick their law into their teeth in order to save
them.

However I have heard that sometimes you have to deal
Devilishly with drowning men in order to swim them to
shore.

Or they will haul themselves and you to the trash and
the fish beneath.

(When I think of this, I do not worry about a few
Chipped teeth.)

It is good I gave glory, it is good I put gold on their
name.

Or there would have been spikes in the afterward hands.

But let us speak only of my success and the pictures in
the Caucasian dailies

As well as the Negro weeklies. For I am a gem.

(They are not concerned that it was hardly The Enemy
my fight was against

But them.)

It was a tall time. And of course my blood was
Boiling about in my head and straining and howling
and singing me on.

Of course I was rolled on wheels of my boy itch to get
at the gun.

Of course all the delicate rehearsal shots of my child-
hood massed in mirage before me.

Of course I was child
And my first swallow of the liquor of battle bleeding
    black air dying and demon noise
Made me wild.

It was kinder than that, though, and I showed like a
    banner my kindness.
I loved. And a man will guard when he loves.
Their white-gowned democracy was my fair lady.
With her knife lying cold, straight, in the softness of
    her sweet-flowing sleeve.
But for the sake of the dear smiling mouth and the
    stuttered promise I toyed with my life.
I threw back!—I would not remember
Entirely the knife.

Still—am I good enough to die for them, is my blood
    bright enough to be spilled,
Was my constant back-question—are they clear
On this? Or do I intrude even now?
Am I clean enough to kill for them, do they wish me to
    kill
For them or is my place while death licks his lips and
    strides to them
In the galley still?

(In a southern city a white man said
Indeed, I'd rather be dead;
Indeed, I'd rather be shot in the head
Or ridden to waste on the back of a flood
Than saved by the drop of a black man's blood.)

Naturally, the important thing is, I helped to save them,
   them and a part of their democracy.
Even if I had to kick their law into their teeth in order
   to do that for them.
And I am feeling well and settled in myself because I
   believe it was a good job,
Despite this possible horror: that they might prefer the
Preservation of their law in all its sick dignity and their
   knives
To the continuation of their creed
And their lives.

HATTIE SCOTT
the end of the day

It's usually from the insides of the door
That I takes my peek at the sun
Pullin' off his clothes and callin' it a day.
'Cause I'm gettin' the dishes done
About that time. Not that I couldn't
Sneak out on the back porch a bit,
But the sun and me's the same, could be:
Cap the job, then to hell with it.

No lollin' around the old work-place
But off, spite of somethin' to see.
Yes, off, until time when the sun comes back.
Then it's wearily back for me.

the date

IF SHE don't hurry up and let me out of here.
Keeps pilin' up stuff for me to do.
I ain't goin' to finish that ironin'.
She got another think comin'. Hey, you.
Whatcha mean talkin' about cleanin' silver?
It's eight o'clock now, you fool.
I'm leavin'. Got somethin' interestin' on my mind.
Don't mean night school.

at the hairdresser's

GIMME an upsweep, Minnie,
With humpteen baby curls.
'Bout time I got some glamour.
I'll show them girls.

Think they so fly a-struttin'
With they wool a-blowin' 'round.
Wait'll they see my upsweep.
That'll jop 'em back on the ground.

Got Madam C. J. Walker's first.
Got Poro Grower next.
Ain't none of 'em worked with me, Min.
But I ain't vexed.

Long hair's out of style anyhow, ain't it?
Now it's tie it up high with curls.
So gimme an upsweep, Minnie.
I'll show them girls.

when I die

No LODGE with banners flappin'
Will follow after me.
But one lone little short man
Dressed all shabbily.

He'll have his buck-a-dozen,
He'll lay them on with care.
And the angels will be watchin',
And kiss him sweetly there.

Then off he'll take his mournin' black,
And wipe his tears away.
And the girls, they will be waitin'.
There's nothin' more to say.

the battle

MOE BELLE JACKSON's husband
Whipped her good last night.
Her landlady told my ma they had
A knock-down-drag-out fight.

I like to think
Of how I'd of took a knife
And slashed all of the quickenin'
Out of his lowly life.

But if I know Moe Belle,
Most like, she shed a tear,
And this mornin' it was probably,
"More grits, dear?"

QUEEN OF THE BLUES

MAME was singing
At the Midnight Club.
And the place was red
With blues.
She could shake her body
Across the floor.
For what did she have
To lose?

She put her mama
Under the ground
Two years ago.
(Was it three?)
She covered that grave
With roses and tears.
(A handsome thing
To see.)

She didn't have any
Legal pa
To glare at her,
To shame
Her off the floor
Of the Midnight Club.
Poor Mame.

She didn't have any
Big brother

To shout
"No sister of mine ! . ."
She didn't have any
Small brother
To think she was everything
Fine.

She didn't have any
Baby girl
With velvet
Pop-open eyes.
She didn't have any
Sonny boy
To tell sweet
Sonny boy lies.

"Show me a man
What will love me
Till I die.
Now show me a man
What will love me
Till I die.
Can't find no such a man
No matter how hard
You try.
Go 'long, baby.
Ain't a true man left
In Chi.

"I loved my daddy.
But what did my daddy

Do?
I loved my daddy.
But what did my daddy
Do?
Found him a brown-skin chicken
What's gonna be
Black and blue.

"I was good to my daddy.
Gave him all my dough.
I say, I was good to my daddy.
I gave him all of my dough.
Scrubbed hard in them white folks'
Kitchens
Till my knees was rusty
And so'."

The M.C. hollered,
"Queen of the blues!
Folks, this is strictly
The queen of the blues!"
She snapped her fingers.
She rolled her hips.
What did she have
To lose?

But a thought ran through her
Like a fire.
"Men don't tip their
Hats to me.
They pinch my arms

And they slap my thighs.
But when has a man
Tipped his hat to me?"

Queen of the blues!
Queen of the blues!
Strictly, strictly,
The queen of the blues!

Men are low down
Dirty and mean.
Why don't they tip
Their hats to a queen?

BALLAD OF PEARL MAY LEE

THEN off they took you, off to the jail,
A hundred hooting after.
And you should have heard me at my house.
I cut my lungs with my laughter,
   Laughter,
   Laughter.
I cut my lungs with my laughter.

They dragged you into a dusty cell.
And a rat was in the corner.
And what was I doing? Laughing still.
Though never was a poor gal lorner,
   Lorner,
   Lorner.
Though never was a poor gal lorner.

The sheriff, he peeped in through the bars,
And (the red old thing) he told you,
"You son of a bitch, you're going to hell!"
'Cause you wanted white arms to enfold you,
   Enfold you,
   Enfold you.
'Cause you wanted white arms to enfold you.

But you paid for your white arms, Sammy boy,
And you didn't pay with money.
You paid with your hide and my heart, Sammy boy,
For your taste of pink and white honey,

Honey,
Honey.
For your taste of pink and white honey.

Oh, dig me out of my don't-despair.
Pull me out of my poor-me.
Get me a garment of red to wear.
You had it coming surely,
  Surely,
  Surely,
You had it coming surely.

At school, your girls were the bright little girls.
You couldn't abide dark meat.
Yellow was for to look at,
Black for the famished to eat.
Yellow was for to look at,
Black for the famished to eat.

You grew up with bright skins on the brain,
And me in your black folks bed.
Often and often you cut me cold,
And often I wished you dead.
Often and often you cut me cold.
Often I wished you dead.

Then a white girl passed you by one day,
And, the vixen, she gave you the wink.
And your stomach got sick and your legs liquefied.
And you thought till you couldn't think.
  You thought,

43

You thought,
You thought till you couldn't think.

I fancy you out on the fringe of town,
The moon an owl's eye minding;
The sweet and thick of the cricket-belled dark,
The fire within you winding . . . .
    Winding,
    Winding . . . .
The fire within you winding.

Say, she was white like milk, though, wasn't she?
And her breasts were cups of cream.
In the back of her Buick you drank your fill.
Then she roused you out of your dream.
In the back of her Buick you drank your fill.
Then she roused you out of your dream.

"You raped me, nigger," she softly said.
(The shame was threading through.)
"You raped me, nigger, and what the hell
Do you think I'm going to do?
    What the hell,
    What the hell
Do you think I'm going to do?

"I'll tell every white man in this town.
I'll tell them all of my sorrow.
You got my body tonight, nigger boy.
I'll get your body tomorrow.
    Tomorrow.
    Tomorrow.
I'll get your body tomorrow."

44

And my glory but Sammy she did! She did!
And they stole you out of the jail.
They wrapped you around a cottonwood tree.
And they laughed when they heard you wail.
   Laughed,
   Laughed.
They laughed when they heard you wail.

And I was laughing, down at my house.
Laughing fit to kill.
You got what you wanted for dinner,
But brother you paid the bill.
   Brother,
   Brother,
Brother you paid the bill.

You paid for your dinner, Sammy boy,
And you didn't pay with money.
You paid with your hide and my heart, Sammy boy,
For your taste of pink and white honey,
   Honey,
   Honey.
For your taste of pink and white honey.

Oh, dig me out of my don't-despair.
Oh, pull me out of my poor-me.
Oh, get me a garment of red to wear.
You had it coming surely.
   Surely.
   Surely.
You had it coming surely.

GAY CHAPS AT THE BAR

souvenir for Staff Sergeant Raymond Brooks and every other soldier

gay chaps at the bar

... and guys I knew in the States, young officers, return from the front crying and trembling. Gay chaps at the bar in Los Angeles, Chicago, New York. . . .

LIEUTENANT WILLIAM COUCH
in the South Pacific

WE KNEW how to order. Just the dash
Necessary. The length of gaiety in good taste.
Whether the raillery should be slightly iced
And given green, or served up hot and lush.
And we knew beautifully how to give to women
The summer spread, the tropics, of our love.
When to persist, or hold a hunger off.
Knew white speech. How to make a look an omen.
But nothing ever taught us to be islands.
And smart, athletic language for this hour
Was not in the curriculum. No stout
Lesson showed how to chat with death. We brought
No brass fortissimo, among our talents,
To holler down the lions in this air.

still do I keep my look, my identity . . .

EACH body has its art, its precious prescribed
Pose, that even in passion's droll contortions, waltzes,
Or push of pain—or when a grief has stabbed,
Or hatred hacked—is its, and nothing else's.
Each body has its pose. No other stock
That is irrevocable, perpetual
And its to keep. In castle or in shack.
With rags or robes. Through good, nothing, or ill.
And even in death a body, like no other
On any hill or plain or crawling cot
Or gentle for the lilyless hasty pall
(Having twisted, gagged, and then sweet-ceased to
    bother),
Shows the old personal art, the look. Shows what
It showed at baseball. What it showed in school.

I HOLD my honey and I store my bread
In little jars and cabinets of my will.
I label clearly, and each latch and lid
I bid, Be firm till I return from hell.
I am very hungry. I am incomplete.
And none can tell when I may dine again.
No man can give me any word but Wait,
The puny light. I keep eyes pointed in;
Hoping that, when the devil days of my hurt
Drag out to their last dregs and I resume
On such legs as are left me, in such heart
As I can manage, remember to go home,
My taste will not have turned insensitive
To honey and bread old purity could love.

looking

You have no word for soldiers to enjoy
The feel of, as an apple, and to chew
With masculine satisfaction. Not "good-by!"
"Come back!" or "careful!" Look, and let him go.
"Good-by!" is brutal, and "come back!" the raw
Insistence of an idle desperation
Since could he favor he would favor now.
He will be "careful!" if he has permission.
Looking is better. At the dissolution
Grab greatly with the eye, crush in a steel
Of study—Even that is vain. Expression,
The touch or look or word, will little avail,
The brawniest will not beat back the storm
Nor the heaviest haul your little boy from harm.

piano after war

ON A snug evening I shall watch her fingers,
Cleverly ringed, declining to clever pink,
Beg glory from the willing keys. Old hungers
Will break their coffins, rise to eat and thank.
And music, warily, like the golden rose
That sometimes after sunset warms the west,
Will warm that room, persuasively suffuse
That room and me, rejuvenate a past.
But suddenly, across my climbing fever
Of proud delight—a multiplying cry.
A cry of bitter dead men who will never
Attend a gentle maker of musical joy.
Then my thawed eye will go again to ice.
And stone will shove the softness from my face.

mentors

For I am rightful fellow of their band.
My best allegiances are to the dead.
I swear to keep the dead upon my mind,
Disdain for all time to be overglad.
Among spring flowers, under summer trees,
By chilling autumn waters, in the frosts
Of supercilious winter—all my days
I'll have as mentors those reproving ghosts.
And at that cry, at that remotest whisper,
I'll stop my casual business. Leave the banquet.
Or leave the ball—reluctant to unclasp her
Who may be fragrant as the flower she wears,
Make gallant bows and dim excuses, then quit
Light for the midnight that is mine and theirs.

the white troops had their orders but the Negroes looked like men

THEY had supposed their formula was fixed.
They had obeyed instructions to devise
A type of cold, a type of hooded gaze.
But when the Negroes came they were perplexed.
These Negroes looked like men. Besides, it taxed
Time and the temper to remember those
Congenital iniquities that cause
Disfavor of the darkness. Such as boxed
Their feelings properly, complete to tags—
A box for dark men and a box for Other—
Would often find the contents had been scrambled.
Or even switched. Who really gave two figs?
Neither the earth nor heaven ever trembled.
And there was nothing startling in the weather.

firstly inclined to take what it is told

THEE sacrosanct, Thee sweet, Thee crystalline,
With the full jewel wile of mighty light—
With the narcotic milk of peace for men
Who find Thy beautiful center and relate
Thy round command, Thy grand, Thy mystic good—
Thee like the classic quality of a star:
A little way from warmth, a little sad,
Delicately lovely to adore—
I had been brightly ready to believe.
For youth is a frail thing, not unafraid.
Firstly inclined to take what it is told,
Firstly inclined to lean. Greedy to give
Faith tidy and total. To a total God.
With billowing heartiness no whit withheld.

"God works in a mysterious way"

BUT often now the youthful eye cuts down its
Own dainty veiling. Or submits to winds.
And many an eye that all its age had drawn its
Beam from a Book endures the impudence
Of modern glare that never heard of tact
Or timeliness, or Mystery that shrouds
Immortal joy: it merely can direct
Chancing feet across dissembling clods.
Out from Thy shadows, from Thy pleasant meadows,
Quickly, in undiluted light. Be glad, whose
Mansions are bright, to right Thy children's air.
If Thou be more than hate or atmosphere
Step forth in splendor, mortify our wolves.
Or we assume a sovereignty ourselves.

love note
I: surely

Surely you stay my certain own, you stay
My you. All honest, lofty as a cloud.
Surely I could come now and find you high,
As mine as you ever were; should not be awed.
Surely your word would pop as insolent
As always: "Why, of course I love you, dear."
Your gaze, surely, ungauzed as I could want.
Your touches, that never were careful, what they were.
Surely—But I am very off from that.
From surely. From indeed. From the decent arrow
That was my clean naïveté and my faith.
This morning men deliver wounds and death.
They will deliver death and wounds tomorrow.
And I doubt all. You. Or a violet.

love note
II: flags

STILL, it is dear defiance now to carry
Fair flags of you above my indignation,
Top, with a pretty glory and a merry
Softness, the scattered pound of my cold passion.
I pull you down my foxhole. Do you mind?
You burn in bits of saucy color then.
I let you flutter out against the pained
Volleys. Against my power crumpled and wan.
You, and the yellow pert exuberance
Of dandelion days, unmocking sun;
The blowing of clear wind in your gay hair;
Love changeful in you (like a music, or
Like a sweet mournfulness, or like a dance,
Or like the tender struggle of a fan).

the progress

AND still we wear our uniforms, follow
The cracked cry of the bugles, comb and brush
Our pride and prejudice, doctor the sallow
Initial ardor, wish to keep it fresh.
Still we applaud the President's voice and face.
Still we remark on patriotism, sing,
Salute the flag, thrill heavily, rejoice
For death of men who too saluted, sang.
But inward grows a soberness, an awe,
A fear, a deepening hollow through the cold.
For even if we come out standing up
How shall we smile, congratulate: and how
Settle in chairs? Listen, listen. The step
Of iron feet again. And again   wild.

Set in Linotype Bodoni
Format by A. W. Rushmore
Manufactured by The Haddon Craftsmen
Published by HARPER & BROTHERS
New York and London